TELL ME ABOUT
WRITERS AND
ILLUSTRATORS

ROBERT LOUIS
STEVENSON

written by
John Malam

Evans

Contact the Author

Tell me what you think about this book.
Write to me at Evans Brothers.
Or e-mail me at: johnmalam@aol.com

Internet information

Find out more about Robert Louis Stevenson:

For children
www.sc.edu/library/spcoll/britlit/rls/rls.html
Website of an illustrated RLS exhibition,
maintained by the University of South
Carolina, USA.

For teachers
www.unibg.it/rls/rls.htm
Comprehensive website of on-line RLS
material, including texts, maintained by
the University of Bergamo, Italy.

VISIT OUR WEBSITE
www.evansbooks.co.uk

Published by Evans Brothers Limited
2A Portman Mansions
Chiltern Street
London W1M 1LE

© Evans Brothers Limited 2001

First published 2001

Printed in Hong Kong

British Library Cataloguing in Publication data.

Malam, John
   Robert Louis Stevenson
   1. Stevenson, Robert Louis, 1850-1894 - Biography - Juvenile
literature 2. Authors, Scottish - 19th century - Biography -
Juvenile literature
   I. Title
   823.8

ISBN 0237522152

Robert Louis Stevenson was a writer. He wrote books and poems for children and adults, and he became very well known. He told exciting adventure stories about bloodthirsty pirates, buried treasure and the wild, stormy sea.

Today, more than 100 years after he died, people all over the world still enjoy reading his books and poems. Some of his books have been made into films. This is his story.

◄ This picture of Robert Louis Stevenson was painted when he was about 42 years old.

▲ A scene from "Treasure Island", one of Robert Louis Stevenson's best-loved books.

Robert Louis Stevenson was born in 1850 in Edinburgh, the capital city of Scotland. He was an only child. His family called him by his second name, Louis, which they pronounced 'Lewis'.

Louis's father and his grandfather were both engineers who built lighthouses. When Louis was growing up, his father spent a lot of time working away from home.

▲ Louis, aged four, with his mother, Margaret.

▶ Louis and his father, Thomas.

The Stevensons lived a comfortable life. As a child, Louis was looked after by a nanny, Alison Cunningham. Louis called her 'Cummy' and she called him 'Lou' or 'My Laddie'. Louis was often ill and 'Cummy' nursed him through his terrible coughs and high fevers. Sometimes she sat by his bed, reading and singing to him. They enjoyed making up stories together.

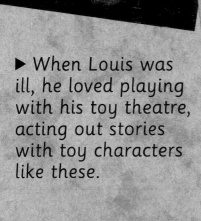

◀ This picture of 'Cummy' was painted when she was an old lady.

▶ When Louis was ill, he loved playing with his toy theatre, acting out stories with toy characters like these.

Louis's many illnesses meant that he could not go to school much. When he did go, he felt awkward. He was very thin, and some of the boys made fun of him. Because he was not strong, Louis could not play sports or join in playground games. But he did have many cousins to play with and he wrote poems about their childhood adventures:

"We built a ship upon the stairs
All made of the back-bedroom chairs."

◄ The house where Louis lived in Edinburgh.

▼ This is how Edinburgh looked when Louis was a child.

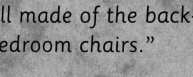

This photo of Louis with his mother and his cousin was taken while they were in Germany.

When Louis was twelve, his family and 'Cummy' went on holiday to France, Italy, Switzerland, Belgium and Germany. They were away for five months. Spending so long abroad must have been a real adventure for Louis.

Louis enjoyed writing, and when he was sixteen he wrote a pamphlet called "The Pentland Rising". It was a story about a real event that happened in Scotland long ago. His father paid for 100 copies of the pamphlet to be printed.

Louis made these sketches on holiday in France.

9

When Louis was seventeen, he went to Edinburgh University to study engineering. His parents were delighted that Louis was going to follow his father and grandfather and be an engineer.

Louis enjoyed university life. He made new friends and had great fun.

▲ At university, Louis dressed in fashionable clothes that made people notice him.

▶ There has been a university in Edinburgh for more than 400 years.

Louis's engineering studies took him to lighthouses all along the rocky coast of Scotland. During these visits he felt the power and danger of the sea. He walked around with a notebook, writing down ideas and describing things he saw.

After three years at university, Louis decided that he did not want to be an engineer after all. His parents, especially his father, were very disappointed. Louis agreed to stay on at university and study law instead of engineering. But in his heart Louis knew what he really wanted to do. He wanted to be a writer.

This photograph was taken after Louis had passed his law exams at university. He is dressed in the wig and gown of an advocate.

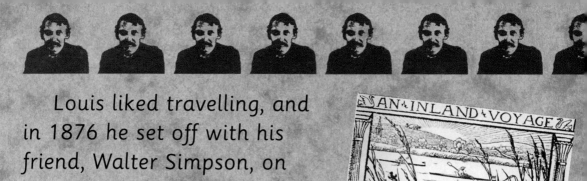

Louis liked travelling, and in 1876 he set off with his friend, Walter Simpson, on a canoe trip. They travelled along the rivers and canals of Belgium and France. Louis made notes about the people he met and the places he visited. He used the notes to write his first book, "An Inland Voyage".

▲ This drawing was printed inside "An Inland Voyage".

◀ Fanny Osbourne. She was ten years older than Louis.

While he was in France, Louis met an American woman called Fanny Osbourne. She was married, but was separated from her husband. Louis fell in love with Fanny.

When Fanny returned to America, Louis went travelling, to try to forget her. He called his next book "Travels With a Donkey". In it he described a walking trip in France, with a donkey called Modestine.

But Louis could not forget Fanny, and in 1879 he travelled all the way to America to see her.

A drawing from "Travels With a Donkey". It shows Louis in his sleeping bag, with Modestine next to him.

Louis's journey to America took two weeks by ship. Then he had to spend another two weeks travelling across the country on a crowded train. It was uncomfortable and made Louis ill. But the journey was worth it. Fanny was now divorced, which meant she was free to marry again.

Louis and Fanny were married in 1880. They did not stay long in America. Instead, together with Fanny's twelve-year-old son, Lloyd, they sailed to Britain.

This drawing is from Louis's book "The Silverado Squatters". It shows him and Fanny on their honeymoon inside a wooden cabin.

In 1881 the family went on holiday to Scotland. The weather was cold and wet, so they had to stay indoors. To pass the time, Lloyd drew a map of an imaginary island. The map gave Louis the idea for a book about pirates and treasure. He wrote it quickly, reading the chapters out loud around the fire at night. The book was "Treasure Island". It was to become one of Louis's most famous books.

► This map was printed in the first edition of "Treasure Island".

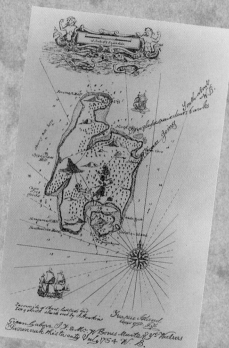

◄ "Treasure Island" is a story about treasure buried on an imaginary island in the Caribbean Sea. The story has been filmed many times for cinema and television.

In 1884 the family moved to Bournemouth, on the south coast of England. Louis still suffered from chest infections and he hoped the sea air would make him feel better.

By now, "Treasure Island" had made Louis a well-known writer.

A painting of Louis and Fanny at their Bournemouth home.

In 1886, while Louis was ill in bed, he wrote "The Strange Case of Dr Jekyll and Mr Hyde". It is the story of a doctor with two personalities — one good, the other bad. In the same year he wrote an adventure story, "Kidnapped". The story is about a boy whose wicked uncle sends him far away from his home in Scotland.

▲ This photograph is from a film of Dr Jekyll and Mr Hyde.

RAIN

THE rain is raining all around,
It falls on field and tree,
It rains on the umbrellas here,
And on the ships at sea.

◄ "A Child's Garden of Verses" has been enjoyed by generations of children.

Louis also wrote poems for children. In his book "A Child's Garden of Verses" there are poems about pirates, travel, foreign lands — and children playing.

Louis had always loved the sea. In 1888 Louis and Fanny, together with Fanny's children, Belle and Lloyd, set off by boat from America. They spent two adventurous years sailing around the islands of the Pacific Ocean. In 1890 they arrived at the island of Upolu, which today is part of Western Samoa. They built a house on the island. Louis loved living there. He spent his time swimming, reading and playing his flageolet (a kind of flute).

The house on Upolu where Louis and his family lived.

◄ In this photograph, Belle is writing down what Louis is saying.

▼ Louis and his friends at a feast.

Louis carried on writing. But he was often ill, so Belle helped him by writing down his words. When he could not speak they used sign language.

Louis loved the people of Samoa and he made many friends there. He enjoyed having picnics and parties. At his birthday party in 1894 there was music, dancing and a feast of food – 804 pineapples, 20 bunches of bananas, 20 pigs, 50 chickens, 17 pigeons and a whole cow!

Shortly before Christmas in 1894, Louis died after a sudden illness. He was buried on Upolu, on Mount Vaea, behind his house. His friends made a path through the jungle. They carried his body up the mountain to his grave.

The people of Samoa called Louis 'Tusitala', which means 'Teller of Tales' or 'The Story Teller'. It is a very good name for a writer who told such exciting stories of mystery and adventure, don't you think?

▼ Robert Louis Stevenson's grave on the island of Upolu.

▲ This portrait of Louis was painted by one of his relatives.

Important dates

1850 Robert Louis Stevenson is born in Scotland

1863 Aged 12 – he goes on his first journey abroad

1866 Aged 16 – he writes a pamphlet called "The Pentland Rising"

1867 Aged 17 – he goes to Edinburgh University

1876 Aged 26 – he goes on a canoe trip to Belgium and France; he meets Fanny Osbourne

1878 Aged 27 – his first book "An Inland Voyage" is published; he goes on a walking trip in France

1879 Aged 28 – his book "Travels With a Donkey" is published; he travels to America

1880 Aged 29 – he marries Fanny Osbourne

1881 Aged 31 – on holiday in Scotland he has the idea for a story about pirates

1883 Aged 33 – his book "Treasure Island" is published

1884 Aged 34 – the family settles in Bournemouth

1885 Aged 35 – his book of poems "A Child's Garden of Verses" is published

1886 Aged 36 – "The Strange Case of Dr Jekyll and Mr Hyde" and "Kidnapped" are published

1888 Aged 37 – he sails in the Pacific Ocean

1890 Aged 39 – he arrives on the island of Upolu in Samoa and builds a house there

1894 Aged 44 – Robert Louis Stevenson dies

Keywords

advocate
a person who works with the law in Scotland

engineer
a person who designs and builds, for example, buildings, bridges, roads or machines

pamphlet
a book with very few pages

sign language
how people 'speak' using their hands to make words

Index